Bible
for children

PEGASUS

www.pegasusforkids.com

Published by Kuldeep Jain for B. Jain Publishers (P) Ltd., D-157, Sector 63, Noida - 201307, U.P

Registered office: 1921/10, Chuna Mandi, Paharganj, New Delhi-110055

Printed in India

Contents

God Creates the World

Thousands of years ago, nothing existed. Only God was there. He was always there. The world on which we live now was formless. It was empty and dark, and was submerged deep in water!

God decided to create a beautiful world. He said, "Let there be light!" Suddenly, a bright light shone through the darkness! God decided to call the light, Day, and the dark, Night. That was the world's very first day!

The next day, God created a dome. He then separated the waters that were under the dome from the waters that were above the dome. The sky became visible. He called the sky, heaven. That was the second day. On the third day, God raised the dry land out of the dark waters. He named the dry land, Earth and the water, Sea. Next, He said, "Let there be plants of every kind." At once, the bare Earth was alive with every kind of grass, flower and fruit bearing tree!

The day after that, God got the sun to brighten the day, and the moon and billions of twinkling stars to shine at night.

On the fifth day, God filled the waters with all kinds of creatures and fishes. Then, he made birds fly in the sky. The birds were of different sizes, shapes, colours and sounds!

The next day, God spoke, "Let there be all kinds of animals on the Earth!" The whole world was now alive with God's creatures, some were huge and others very small. Finally, God made the first Man in His own image, from the dust of the Earth. God was very pleased with all He had made. God took only six days to make everything. He rested on the seventh day.

7

The First Human Beings

God created a lovely garden and named it Eden. It was a paradise abundant with many wonderful things. A great variety of fruit-bearing trees grew there. Many beautiful flowers bloomed everywhere, animals roamed fearlessly and streams flowed through the garden. It was a peaceful, happy place!

God had formed the first man from the dust of the Earth and named him Adam. He asked Adam to take care of the garden. Two unique

trees, the 'Tree of Life' and the 'Tree of the Knowledge of Good and Evil' stood in the middle of the garden.

God told Adam that he could eat the fruits of any tree except the 'Tree of the Knowledge of Good and Evil'.

"You will die if you ever eat its fruit!" he warned.

After some time, God saw that Adam was lonely. So He put Adam into a deep sleep and used a rib from his chest to create the world's first Woman. Adam was so happy to see a female companion that he called her Eve, meaning 'mother of all living things'. They obeyed God's instructions and lived happily in the garden.

The First Sin

But the happiness of Adam and Eve was short-lived! Together with them, there also lived a cunning serpent.

One day, the serpent asked Eve whether God had told them not to eat any fruit from the garden. Eve replied that they would die if they ate the fruit of the 'Tree of the Knowledge of Good and Evil'.

The serpent laughed. "You silly woman, you won't die. Rather you will become wise like God!"

Eve fell into the serpent's trap! She forgot how kind and good God was, and ate the forbidden fruit. She even encouraged Adam to eat it. Soon, they understood that they were not clothed, and covered themselves in fig leaves!

When God came, Adam and Eve hid in fear. God asked them if they had eaten the forbidden fruit. Adam blamed Eve who in turn accused the serpent of tricking her.

God was very angry with Adam and Eve for disobeying Him! He banished them from the garden.

From that day on, Adam would have to work hard to make a living. Eve would suffer pain while having children and raising them.

He also punished the serpent by cursing him to always crawl on the ground and be an enemy of Human beings and their children.

This is how sin came between God and His children.

The First Brothers

After being thrown out of Eden for disobeying God, Adam and Eve started their life on the Earth. In time, God blessed them with two sons, Cain and Abel. Cain grew up to become a farmer while Abel was a shepherd.

One day, Cain and Abel decided to give offerings to God. Cain picked up fruits and vegetables for God. Abel brought his best lamb as a sacrifice. God saw that Abel really wanted to please and thank Him, so God respected his sacrifice.

God told an angry Cain that if he followed God's instructions, his offering too would be accepted. He also warned Cain that sin was waiting to destroy him and he should control it.

But Cain did not listen to God. Instead, his hatred for Abel grew. One day, when they were both in a field, Cain killed Abel. When God asked Cain where Abel was, Cain answered, "Am I my brother's keeper?"

God was angry. He cursed Cain for killing his brother. The ground would no longer produce fruit and vegetables if Cain tried to grow them. He would have to live as a wanderer forever!

Cain felt his punishment was too difficult and also that his life would be in danger. So, God put a mark upon his forehead, so that no one could ever kill Cain.

Cleansing the World

When God first created the world, everything was perfect. But all that changed when Adam and Eve disobeyed Him. Abel's murder was the beginning of violence and wickedness in the world. People forgot God. The world was becoming a terrible place to live in!

God was very unhappy to see His beautiful world spoilt in this way. He felt sorry for having created Man. So He decided to destroy all His creation and start a fresh.

However, there was a good man named Noah who always obeyed God. One day, God told Noah about His plan to wipe humankind off the face of the Earth with a flood.

"Build a mighty ark from good timber and put rooms in it. Cover it with tar inside and out. Build it with three decks and put a door in the side. Everything on the Earth will be destroyed, but I am going to make a special arrangement for you," God told Noah.

Noah did just as God had instructed him to do. However, the people mocked Noah. They had never ever seen a boat! But Noah ignored their jibes. At last, the ark was ready!

God spoke again, "Noah, take your wife, your sons and their wives into the ark. Also bring on board a male and female of every kind of animal and bird. Of some, take seven pairs; of others, just one pair. Do this so that every species will survive and will bear young ones on Earth again!"

Noah brought in seven of every type of clean animals and two of every unclean animal.

Once they were all in, God shut the door of the ark.

Noah's Ark

Despite God's repeated warnings, people chose not to repent for their sins. So God decided to get rid of everything He had created.

Until then, it had never rained upon the Earth. Noah, his family and all the creatures He had chosen were in the ark. Then, seven days later, the great flood came!

Water poured from the sky, and rushed up from the ground. The ark began to float. The rain continued for forty days! Soon, the water covered the mountaintops. Every living creature that lived on the Earth died. Only those who took shelter in Noah's ark were safe!

The water flooded the Earth for a hundred and fifty days! Then God sent a wind to aid the waters go down. Slowly and gradually, the floodwaters started to ebb. Finally, Noah's ark came to rest on a mountaintop known as Ararat.

One evening, Noah opened a window and sent out a dove to see if the Earth had dried completely or not. It returned with a fresh olive leaf in its beak. He waited another week, and then sent the dove out again. This time, the dove did not return.

God told Noah that it was time for his family and the animals to leave the ark. At once, Noah built an altar and offered a sacrifice of the clean animals. God was pleased. He blessed Noah.

God put a beautiful rainbow in the sky, promising Noah that He would never again destroy the Earth with water. Until the Earth remains, there will always be seeds and harvest, cold and heat, winter and summer, day and night.

The Origin of Languages

After the great flood, God had commanded Noah and his family to spread out all over the world. Instead, Noah's descendants settled in the land of Shinar. At that time, everyone spoke the same language.

Time passed, and the people discovered how to make bricks and use tar to hold them together. They began to feel that they could do anything they wanted. Their pride made them turn against God, again!

One day, the people decided to build a huge tower, as high as heaven! They thought that by doing so, they would soon become powerful and the envy of the other people. They would no longer have to disperse to various places throughout the world either.

They began building the tower. When God saw what the people were up to, He became very sad and angry. He knew that once the tower was made, there would be no end to greed, envy and scheming. He decided to teach the people a lesson!

Instead of knocking down the tower, God changed their language to confuse them. All of a sudden, each one spoke words the others could not understand! Soon, they quit building the tower. God then made them spread out across the earth.

This is why there are so many different languages in the world today!

The Man who obeyed God's Call

One of Noah's descendants was Abraham. He was a rich shepherd who lived with his wife Sarah in the land of Haran. But he had no children.

Abraham was a good man, and had been a loyal servant of God all his life. God was pleased with him and chose him to lead the beginning of a new nation.

When Abraham was seventy-five years old, God appeared before him and said, "Leave your land immediately and go live in the land that I show you. I will bless you and your wife Sarah!"

Abraham trusted God, so he soon left Haran with his wife, servants, nephew, Lot, and his sheep and goats. He took with him everything that belonged to him, in search of the land God had instructed him to find. They set off towards Canaan and only stopped for water.

Soon, they reached the holy place of Shecham. There, God again appeared in front of Abraham and said, "Look around, I give this land to you and your descendants. Look up at the stars in the sky, I promise you, one day your descendants will be as many."

Abraham was worried because he and Sarah were too old to have children. But nothing was impossible for God, so Abraham continued to have faith in Him.

Within a few months, they had their first son, and they called him Isaac.

Abraham's Big Test

Isaac's birth brought great joy to the lives of Abraham and Sarah. They thanked and praised God for keeping His promise. They brought up Isaac according to God's commands.

A few years passed. God wanted to see if Abraham was still loyal to Him. So he appeared before Abraham and said, "Abraham, offer your son Isaac to me as sacrifice on the mountain that I will show you."

Abraham was shocked, but he trusted God. He saddled up a donkey and with the help of his two servants, took his son and some chopped wood to the mountain God had showed him.

After reaching the mountain, he dismissed his two servants and prepared an altar. His son asked him, "Father, I see the preparations are for a sacrifice, but who is to be sacrificed?"

Abraham smiled at his son and said, "Don't worry, son. God will provide one." He then tied up Isaac and laid him on top of the chopped wood. As he took a knife to kill his son, an angel appeared before him.

The angel said, "Wait Abraham! Do not harm the child. The Lord was just testing you to see if you are still faithful. But now He knows that you would do anything for Him, even sacrifice your only son!"

Relieved, Abraham looked around and saw a ram stuck in a thicket. He took the ram and offered it, instead of his son, to God.

A Bride for Isaac

Abraham wanted his son Isaac to marry a woman who loved God. So he sent his oldest servant to bring a wife for Isaac from his family in Mesopotamia.

The servant started his journey. When he came to the place where Abraham once lived, he stopped by a well to rest. It was evening, the time when the women there would come to fill their water pitchers.

The servant prayed to God to help him find a suitable bride for Isaac. Finally, he decided to ask for a drink at the well, and the woman who would offer water to his camels as well would be the one chosen by God to be Isaac's wife.

Even before he could finish his prayers, a beautiful woman came to fill her pitcher at the well. The servant asked her, "Can I have some water to drink?" The woman replied, "Yes, you can. I will bring water for your camels also."

At once, the servant knew that this was the woman he was sent to look for.

The beautiful woman's name was Rebekah. The servant told her about Isaac and asked her if she would like to come with him to Canaan. She gladly agreed.

With her father's blessings, Rebekah set out for Canaan. Isaac was praying in the field when he saw the camels coming back. He immediately ran towards his bride. He took Rebekah as his wife and loved her all his life.

Jacob is Abraham's Heir

After twenty years of marriage, God blessed Isaac and Rebekah with twin boys. The elder son was named Esau and the younger Jacob. Esau was hairy and red skinned, and fond of hunting. In contrast, Jacob was quiet and wise. He preferred to stay at home and take care of his father's flock. Esau was Isaac's favourite son, while Jacob was Rebekah's.

In those times, the birthright was a sacred right enjoyed by the firstborn son. So Esau would inherit a double portion of Isaac's possessions than Jacob. But Esau never cared about his birthright or the blessing that God had promised. On the contrary, Jacob yearned for the inheritance rights!

Soon, Jacob got the opportunity to gain the birthright for himself. One day, Esau came home tired and hungry. Jacob asked Esau to swap his birthright for some bread and a bowl of lentil stew!

Many years passed. Isaac became very old and could no longer see. He felt that the time had come for him to give his elder son Esau a special blessing. He asked Esau to prepare a tasty meal of wild meat, and receive the blessing. Esau, however, did not tell his father that he had sold his birthright to Jacob!

Now, Rebekah who overheard their conversation instructed Jacob to quickly get two goat kids. She cooked the goat meat in a special way that Isaac liked. Rebekah then took the hair of the kids and covered Jacob's arms and neck to resemble Esau's hairy skin.

Wearing Esau's clothes, Jacob went into his father's tent with the meal. "Who is it?" asked Isaac. "I am Esau," answered Jacob. "I have brought your meal." Isaac asked Jacob to come near him. After touching and smelling Jacob, he was still confused. He said, "The voice sounds like Jacob, but the hands are like Esau's. Are you really Esau?" Jacob lied again, "I am, father."

Satisfied, Isaac ate the meal and blessed Jacob. Shortly after, Esau arrived with the meal only to discover that Jacob had robbed him again. Esau was so angry that he wanted to kill Jacob! Isaac was sad too; but it was too late.

Jacob, had to pay a price for stealing his brother's blessing he had to leave his family!

Thus, it was Jacob whom God had chosen to become Abraham's heir, as revealed to Rebekah!

Jacob Reunites with Esau

Jacob set out on the journey to Haran where his uncle Laban lived. That night, he slept on the ground with a large stone as pillow. He dreamt of angels going up and down a shiny stairway that reached the heaven. He also saw God standing at the top!

God promised Jacob that He would give the very land he was sleeping on to him and his descendants. He also promised Jacob that He would be with him always.

Early next morning, Jacob took the stone, used as pillow, set it up as a pillar, poured oil on it and called the place Bethel or House of God. Jacob also promised to serve God all his life and vowed to give Him one-tenth of all his wealth.

Jacob later married his uncle Laban's daughters, Leah and Rachel, and stayed in Haran for a long time. After twenty years, God commanded Jacob to return to his native land, Canaan. He was eager to meet his father Isaac, who was still alive, and make peace with his brother Esau. So, along with his entire family, servants and livestock, he set off on his journey.

When Jacob heard that Esau was coming with four hundred men, he was struck with fear. He divided his family and belongings into two parts. He then prayed to God to help him. After that, he sent a gift— hundreds of animals—to Esau. That evening, he sent all his family and everything he owned across the Jabbok brook. He stayed alone on the other side of the brook to pray.

Suddenly, a stranger came and started wrestling with him. Jacob and the stranger wrestled all night. Finally, they stopped. But Jacob was not willing to give up until the stranger agreed to bless him, even after straining his thigh! The stranger changed Jacob's name to Israel, meaning one who struggled with God and won. At that moment, Jacob realised that he had wrestled with God all night!

Early next morning, Esau came to meet Jacob. He ran and hugged Jacob happily. Esau had forgiven his brother for all the wrong that he had done.

As Jacob was also called Israel, all his descendants were called Israelites. Meanwhile, Esau, his children and his cattle went away to a land in the southeast of Canaan, called Edom.

Joseph's Brothers Sell Him

Jacob had twelve sons from his two wives Leah and Rachel. Of all his children, his second youngest son Joseph was the apple of his eye.

Joseph received a special gift from his father when he turned seventeen, a long-sleeved coat made of many colours! This was a privilege usually given to the firstborn. So the older sons became jealous.

Joseph was a dreamer. One night, he had a strange dream. He told his brothers about how he had dreamt that they were tying the stalks of wheat, when suddenly their stalks of wheat stood around his stalk and bowed down! His brothers clearly understood the dream's significance. They felt deeply insulted. They could not imagine Joseph ruling over them! Matters between the brothers became worse.

Not long after, Joseph dreamt that the sun, the moon and eleven stars were all bowing to him. The next morning, he shared the dream with his brothers in the presence of his father. An angry Jacob scolded Joseph. But he secretly wondered whether God was going to make Joseph a very great person when he grew up.

One day, Joseph's brothers were away, tending their flock in some far away pastures. Jacob sent Joseph to check on them. The brothers spotted him walking towards them wearing the special coat. They plotted to get rid of him. But the oldest brother, Reuben, convinced them to throw Joseph into a nearby dry well. Reuben planned to rescue him later. The others agreed. They snatched the special coat from Joseph, and threw him into the well. Later, when Reuben was not around, they sold him to some Midianite traders for 20 pieces of silver!

The brothers returned home and showed Joseph's coat to Jacob. They had soaked the coat in a goat's blood. Jacob cried and mourned for his beloved son.

Joseph, the Dream Decoder

Joseph was his father's favourite son. But one day, his entire life changed when his jealous brothers sold him as a slave to some travelling traders.

The traders took Joseph to Egypt and sold him to a powerful officer of the Pharaoh, named Potiphar. Potiphar saw God was with Joseph, and soon made him his trusted assistant. From that day, God blessed Potiphar's house and everything he owned.

But, Joseph soon found himself in trouble. Potiphar's wife had taken a liking to Joseph. When Joseph refused to do what she wanted, Potiphar's wife complained to her husband and made false charges against Joseph. Potiphar believed his wife and threw Joseph into the royal prison.

But God, who had already blessed Joseph with a unique gift to interpret dreams, did not forget him. Soon, the jailor saw that Joseph was honest and put him in charge of the other prisoners.

Time went by. One night, two prisoners— the Pharaoh's butler and baker— had strange dreams. Joseph told them the meaning of their dreams. He said the butler would be restored to his position while the baker would be executed, all in three days. Both the interpretations came true! However, the butler forgot about Joseph and never mentioned him to the Pharaoh.

Two years later, the Pharaoh had two disturbing dreams. None of the magicians and wise men of Egypt could interpret them. Suddenly, the butler remembered Joseph! At once, he told the Pharaoh about Joseph. Joseph was quickly summoned to the palace.

Joseph listened to the Pharaoh's dreams. He then told the ruler that the two dreams were the same. "This is God's warning. There will be seven years of abundance followed by seven years of severe drought!" he revealed.

Joseph's Rise to Prominence

God had great plans for Joseph, and was just waiting for the perfect time. For this reason, He made the Pharaoh to have two disturbing dreams. With God's help, Joseph interpreted those dreams. He also advised the Pharaoh to appoint a wise man to see to it that surpluses were stored and preserved during the good years. "This will help people survive the drought," he added.

The Pharaoh was pleased with Joseph's wise advice. He said, "You are the one who fits the bill. Therefore, I appoint you as my second-in-command." Joseph was speechless! Then, Joseph was given jewels, servants and a beautiful house to live in.

Joseph was loyal to God and the Pharaoh. He travelled all over Egypt and gave orders to construct huge storehouses to hold the extra grains. For the next seven years, the storehouses were filled up with so much grain that Joseph stopped keeping record of it.

Meanwhile, Joseph married a noblewoman and had two sons. Finally, the famine came. Egypt had plenty and the famished people from all the surrounding countries came to Joseph to buy grains. Among them were Joseph's older brothers! Joseph recognised them, but they did not know who he was.

When Joseph accused them of spying, his brothers revealed their true identity. "Bring your younger brother to prove your innocence. Till then, let one among you remain here," said Joseph. Simeon was chosen to stay behind. Joseph then filled the other brothers' sacks with grains along with the money they paid for it. The brothers left for Canaan with a heavy heart.

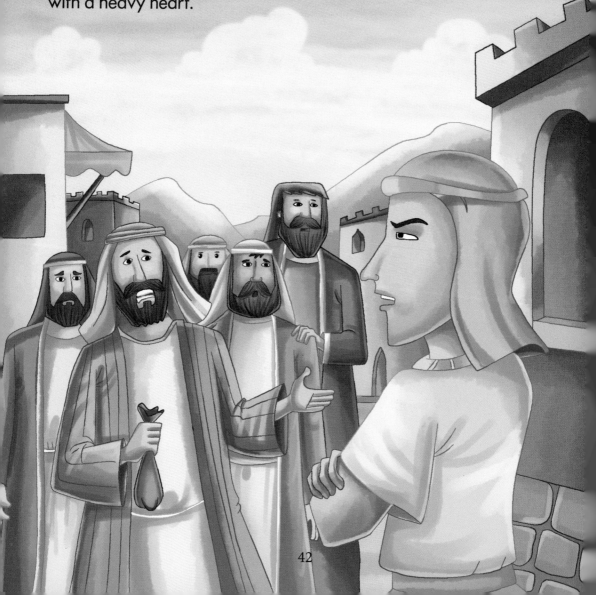

Jacob Meets His Long Lost Son

Joseph had not seen his brothers since they had sold him as a slave. But when they turned up in Egypt to buy grains during the severe drought, he immediately recognised them.

Ten of Joseph's brothers had come to Egypt, but only nine returned back. Joseph wanted to test whether his brothers had repented from their earlier sin. He held Simeon as hostage, to check whether his brothers would leave him in prison, or return as they promised.

Back home, the brothers explained to their father, Jacob, what had happened in Egypt. "A powerful official of Egypt wants to see Benjamin. Otherwise, Simeon will stay in prison," said Reuben. But Jacob refused to let Benjamin go with them.

When their supply of food eventually ran out, Jacob reluctantly agreed to send Benjamin to Egypt. When Joseph saw his brothers returning, he told his servant to prepare a special meal for them.

On their way back to Canaan with a fresh supply of grains, Joseph's brothers were accused of stealing Joseph's silver cup. Joseph's servant found the cup in Benjamin's sack. The horrified brothers silently followed the servant back to Egypt.

When his brother, Judah, pleaded with Joseph to make him his slave instead of his little brother, Joseph understood that his brothers had indeed changed. He could not keep his identity a secret anymore!

Joseph ordered his servants to leave the room. Once alone, Joseph said, "I am Joseph, your long lost brother!" The brothers were too stunned to reply. Joseph hugged them and kissed them. He also explained that he was not angry with them. He had already forgiven them for what they had done.

Old Jacob was overjoyed when he heard the news. Soon, the large family of Jacob went to Egypt. What a happy sight it was when Jacob met Joseph!

The Prince from River

Over time, there were thousands and thousands of Israelites living in Egypt. These people, who were the descendants of Jacob, were also called Hebrews.

However, the new Pharaoh of Egypt forgot about the good things that Joseph had done for his kingdom. All he knew was that the Israelites were growing in number and were a serious threat to him. So, the Pharaoh ordered that all newborn Hebrew baby boys be thrown into the River Nile! He also made the Israelites his slaves.

During this horrible time, an Israelite couple had a baby boy. His mother set him afloat in a reed basket on the river, and asked her daughter Miriam to watch over her baby brother.

Soon, the baby's cradle floated into the river where the Pharaoh's daughter bathed. The Pharaoh's daughter was a kind woman. She decided to keep the baby.

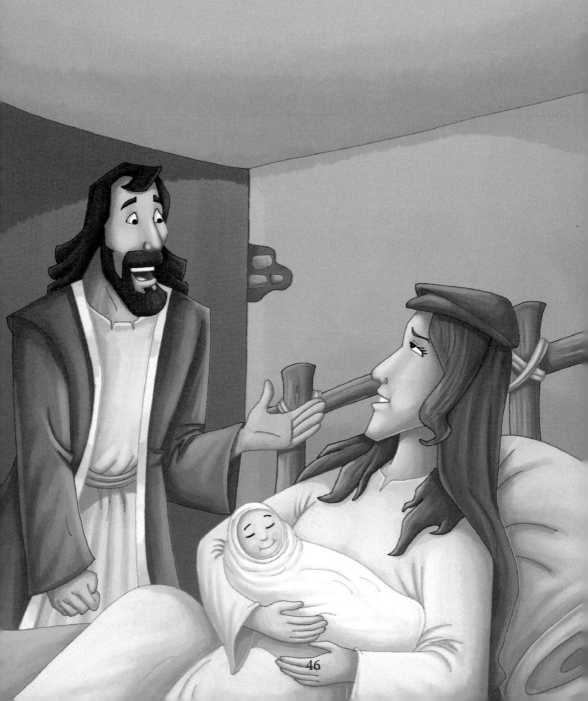

On Miriam's suggestion, the Pharaoh's daughter appointed the baby's own mother to nurse and raise the baby.

The Hebrew baby, who was named Moses, grew up as an Egyptian prince. But he never forgot his people and God.

One day, Moses killed an Egyptian who had unmercifully beaten one of his Jewish brethren. Scared of the Pharaoh's wrath, he fled to Midian.

47

The Saviour of Israelites

In Midian, Moses met a shepherd-priest named Jethro and married his daughter. He too became a shepherd and settled there.

One day, Moses took his flock to Mount Horeb. There, he saw something amazing that changed his whole life! He came across a bush on fire, but it was not spreading. Curious, Moses went to take a closer look. Suddenly, the voice of God called to him.

God explained to Moses that He had picked him to rescue His chosen people, the Israelites, from slavery. Moses was terrified, but he listened to God and agreed to meet the Pharaoh.

On the way to Egypt, Moses met his brother Aaron, as God had promised. After reaching Egypt, the brothers went to the Pharaoh to

ask him to set the Israelites free. But the Pharaoh was not willing to lose his slaves. He made the slaves work even harder. If they failed to do their task properly, they were ruthlessly beaten up.

The Israelites now blamed Moses for their predicament. God asked Moses and Aaron to meet the Pharaoh again. This time, they did exactly as God had commanded them. Aaron threw his stick to the ground and it turned into a big snake. The Pharaoh's sorcerers and magicians also did the same thing. But Aaron's snake gobbled up the other snakes! The Pharaoh still did not release the Israelites.

God decided to teach the Pharaoh a lesson. Terrible things began to happen in Egypt.

Israelites No Longer Slaves

Moses and Aaron again approached the Pharaoh on the banks of the river Nile. They warned him about God's punishment if he did not heed to God. But the Pharaoh refused to set the Israelites free.

So God struck Egypt with plagues, each one worse than the last. But before each one, God warned the Pharaoh through Moses.

First was the plague of blood. Aaron struck the Nile with his staff. The next moment, all the water in the kingdom turned to blood! All the

fishes in the river died and a terrible foul smell spread all over. Only the Israelites were spared. Still, the Pharaoh did not give in.

After due warnings to the Pharaoh, God sent the plague of frogs, followed by the plague of lice and fleas, and the plague of a great swarm of flies. The fifth plague was a terrible disease that massacred the Egyptian livestock. Then, the plague of boils broke out on the men and animals.

The next plague came in the form of the worst hailstorm in the history of Egypt! It destroyed all the crops growing in Egypt. The eighth plague of locusts ate up everything. Then, ninth plague of darkness lasted in Egypt for three days. But still the Pharaoh held the Israelites as his slaves. During this time, the God's people were saved from any harm!

Finally, God sent the worst plague to Egypt. That night, the eldest son in every Egyptian family, including the Pharaoh's son, died. The Israelites obeyed God's instructions, so they were not affected. The Pharaoh was so upset that he ordered the Israelites to leave Egypt immediately.

After four hundred and thirty years of slavery, the Israelites were finally free! That day was known as the Passover. From that day on, the Israelites keep a holy feast in honour of God, every year.

But everything was not over. The Pharaoh chased the Israelites with his army. God parted the Red Sea and allowed His people to pass safely. He drowned the Pharaoh and his army under the sea. God also provided His people with water from a rock, manna and quail from heaven while they wandered in the wilderness for forty years!

Finally, He wanted to set His people apart from the pagan nations around them. So He gave them His word in the form of the Tablets of the Ten Commandments to be obeyed.

A Talking Donkey Saves Greedy Master

Balak, the king of Moab, was terrified to see the Israelites marching towards his kingdom. He thought of ways to defeat them. He suddenly remembered about Balaam who had unusual powers he could utter blessing or curses with powerful outcome! So he summoned Balaam to cast an evil spell on the Israelites.

Balaam was offered money for the task. But God warned Balaam against cursing His people. So Balaam sent Balak's messengers back. Balak tried again. This time, he sent the princes and promised Balaam more money! Balaam still refused, he did not wish to anger God.

The princes decided to stay with Balaam. That night, God gave Balaam permission to go to Moab but on one condition he was to speak only what God told him to say! The next day, Balaam started his journey. But God knew that Balaam was greedy for money. He sent an angel to stop Balaam. The donkey saw the angel. Balaam did not see the angel, so he was furious when his donkey suddenly ran off to the field. He caught and hit the donkey. But, the donkey stamped on Balaam's foot! An angry Balaam hit the donkey again. Next, the donkey lay down on the road! Balaam hit it a third time. Suddenly, God made the donkey talk! It asked Balaam why he beat it three times. "You made me look like a fool," replied Balaam. Just then, God opened Balaam's eyes. He saw the angel! The angel told Balaam to bless the Israelites, instead of cursing them!

When Balaam met King Balak, he did not curse the Israelites. Instead, he blessed them and talked about how good God was. Balak's plan to curse the Israelites had backfired.

How Jericho was Captured

After the death of Moses, Joshua was put in charge of the Israelite people. And the city of Jericho was the first test of his leadership!

Jericho, situated across the river Jordan, was surrounded by a thick, high wall around it. The people there had rejected God and were quite confident that no enemy could ever sneak in or out of their city. But nothing was impossible for God!

Joshua sent out two spies to find out about Jericho's defences. The spies reached Jericho and stayed in the house of a woman called Rahab. The king of Jericho sent his soldiers to capture the spies.

Rahab had faith in God, so she hid the Israelite spies under flax stalks on her roof. The soldiers could not find the spies, so they left.

In return for her kindness, the spies promised to save Rahab and her family. They told her to hang a red cord out of her window so that her house would be spared.

The spies returned and told Joshua all that they had learnt. But how were the people supposed to cross the flooded River Jordan? God intervened. He rolled back the waters of the river and helped the Israelites cross the river safely. Joshua set up a memorial with twelve stones from the riverbed to mark the occasion.

The walls of Jericho stood towering before the Israelites. But God told Joshua how to conquer the city. For six days, the Israelite soldiers marched silently around the city once a day. Seven priests blew their trumpets. On the seventh day, they marched around the city seven times. On the seventh time, Joshua asked the Israelites to blow the trumpets and shout as loudly as they could. The mighty walls of Jericho fell down flat! As promised, Rahab's house was spared.

A Woman of Faith and Courage

For about three hundred years, the Israelites had no kings. Instead, they had men or women chosen by God from time to time to lead them. These 'judges' helped them to serve God and often led them in battles.

One such judge was a woman prophet named Deborah. She sat under the shade of a palm tree where the Israelites often came for judgment.

At that time, the Israelites were under the control of the Canaanite king, Jabin. For twenty years, Jabin and his cruel army commander, Sisera, terrorised the Israelites. So the Israelites turned to God again and prayed for help.

God heard their prayer and told Deborah what to do. At once, she summoned a brave warrior named Barak and told him that he was chosen by God to fight against Sisera's army. Barak, however, was reluctant to go without Deborah! She warned him, "I will go with you. You didn't believe in God, so the credit for the victory will not be yours but mine!"

Deborah and Barak, along with an army of ten thousand men, marched toward Mount Tabor. Meanwhile, Sisera came with nine hundred iron chariots into battle against the Israelites.

But God was with Barak, and troubled Sisera's army by sending rain. Every single soldier was killed. Sisera jumped from his chariot and escaped on foot. As he ran, he saw some tents near the valley. These tents belonged to Kenites, a nomadic clan who was friendly with King Jabin.

Sisera ran to the tent of Jael, the wife of Heber. She invited him in, gave him some milk to drink, and asked him lie down on a mat. When he was asleep, she took a tent peg and hammered it through Sisera's temple. Sisera was killed instantly!

When Barak came looking for Sisera, he saw the dead man. Later, Barak and the army destroyed King Jabin and freed Israel.

Winning an Impossible Battle

With God's help, the Israelites were able to conquer the Promised Land of Canaan. But over time, they turned away from Him, and began worshipping idols. This made God angry. So he let the strong cruel tribesmen, the Midianites, to rule over them.

For seven years, the Midianites invaded the land of Israelites and destroyed their crops and livestock. The Israelites hid in the caves of the mountains. They had no option but to turn to God again for help.

God chose a poor farmer's son named Gideon to lead the Israelites against the wicked Midianites. Gideon knew that he could not defeat the Midianites by himself. But when assured of God's direction and protection, he took up the task. Gideon and his ten servants destroyed the false altars, built an altar for God, and made a burnt offering to God.

He then gathered thousands of men for the battle. But God asked him to take only three hundred men. He did this because He wanted the Israelites to acknowledge that it was His strength that won the battle and not theirs!

Gideon feared that the soldiers would not be enough to defeat the mighty raiders. But he trusted God. He decided to attack the Midianites' camp in the night. He gave each of his soldiers a trumpet and a torch hidden in a jug.

As night dawned, the army of Gideon got ready to attack. On his signal, the soldiers broke the jugs and sounded the trumpets. All the noise and the lights confused the Midianites. They fled in terror, never to return.

The Strongest Man on Earth

The Israelites, once again, sinned and turned away from God. So, He decided to use the Philistines to punish them!

Now, an Israelite man called Manoah and his wife were loyal to God. They had longed for a child of their own. One day, an angel of God appeared before Manoah's wife and said, "You will soon have a son. He will save Israel from the Philistines. But he should never cut his hair, drink alcohol or touch dead things all his life. He shall be a Nazirite to the Lord."

The wonderful boy was Samson. When Samson grew up, God blessed him with extraordinary strength. He was so strong that he killed a lion with his bare hands and a thousand Philistines with a donkey's jawbone! The Philistines hated Samson, but they could not harm him.

Time passed. Samson did not always follow God's laws. The Israelites were forbidden from marrying foreigners. But Samson decided to marry a certain Philistine girl.

On his way to the wedding, Samson passed the carcass of a lion. To his surprise, inside it was a swarm of wild bees and lots of honey! Samson ate some of the honey and went to the wedding venue. Samson got married to his Philistine bride.

At his week-long wedding celebrations, Samson posed a riddle based on the honey and lion to his Philistine attendants. He promised them rich rewards if they correctly answered his riddle within seven days.

However, the puzzled Philistines could not solve the riddle! They threatened Samson's wife and her family with their lives if she did not find out the answer to the riddle.

On the last day of the feast, the Philistines answered Samson's riddle. He understood that his wife had betrayed him. Samson was furious. He stormed off the celebrations, planning revenge.

From that day, Samson started carrying out attacks against the Philistines. For many years, Samson attacked the Philistines single-handedly. The Philistines tried to capture Samson in vain. Samson, the Israelite champion, was too strong to be bound in ropes and chains!

The Fall of Mighty Samson

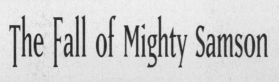

Samson's real trouble started when he fell in love with a Philistine woman named Delilah. When the Philistine rulers learnt about this, they offered Delilah a large amount of money to discover the secret of Samson's strength.

Delilah was a greedy woman. So she coaxed Samson to tell her the secret behind his strength. At first, he told her that he would become weak if anyone tied him up with seven fresh bowstrings.

Delilah tied him up with seven fresh bowstrings while he was asleep. She then shouted, "Samson, the Philistines are here!" Samson woke up and snapped those strings.

Delilah tried to trick Samson two more times. But both times, he escaped! By now, Delilah was desperate to know Samson's secret. She pleaded to Samson every day until he could no longer stand her nagging. He said, "My strength is in my hair. As long as I don't shave it, no one can defeat me."

That was Samson's biggest mistake! Delilah had a man shave off Samson's hair while he slept. When Samson awoke, he found he had lost his strength. The Philistines blinded him and imprisoned him. But, soon enough, Samson's hair began to grow again.

One day, the Philistines organised a great feast in the temple of their god. The temple and the roof over it were crowded with more than three thousand men and women. They brought Samson there and bound him between two pillars. Samson repented his sins and asked God to give him the strength once more to destroy his enemy.

Then, Samson pushed forward with all his might, and brought down the temple! Samson himself was among the thousands who were dead.

The Blessings of Loyalty

Ruth was not one of God's chosen people, but a Moabite. At that time, Moabites were long-time enemies of the Israelites. Yet, she forsake her pagan heritage and values to follow one living God.

Once, a severe famine forced an Israelite man named Elimelech to leave Judah and live in the land of Moab with his wife Naomi, and two sons. While living there, Elimelech died. His two sons grew up, and married from Moab. Some years later, the sons too died.

Naomi decided to return to Bethlehem after hearing that the famine was over. When Naomi asked her daughters-in-law to go their own way, one of them, Ruth, refused to leave her. She could not bear to be apart from Naomi or from the God of Israel. Naomi was very happy that Ruth was coming with her.

The two women reached Bethlehem just in time when the barley harvest was in full swing. Ruth immediately went to work in the fields to support herself and her mother-in-law.

While she worked, the field owner named Boaz came by. He was a man of good character, and a relative of Naomi. Boaz noticed Ruth's hard work. So he told the reapers to leave some extra grains behind for her to pick.

Boaz also asked Ruth to stay with his maidens and glean in his field throughout the harvest. Ruth was overcome with gratitude. She believed that God was faithful to those who walked in His ways.

And God indeed blessed Ruth's faithfulness. Boaz married Ruth at the end of the harvest. God blessed them with a son, Obed, who was the grandfather of King David! So Ruth, who was not an Israelite, became part of the family line in which Jesus Himself was born.

David, the Giant Slayer

David was a young shepherd boy who believed in God. His destiny changed when Prophet Samuel anointed him as the successor of King Saul. However, he was not to take the throne immediately.

David continued to take care of his father's sheep. At that time, the Israelites and the Philistines were still waging a war against each other. David's three older brothers fought for King Saul.

Now it so happened that every day a nine-feet-tall Philistine giant named Goliath challenged the Israelites'

camp to fight with him. He was protected from head to toe by armour, and was armed with a sword and spear.

"Choose one of your men, and send him to fight with me. If I kill him, then all of you will serve us and if he kills me, then we will be your servants," he would shout every day. This continued for forty days! But no man in the Israelite army dared to fight the giant.

One day, when David came to meet his brothers, he heard Goliath mocking God and His army. He was furious. He decided to kill this proud giant. Soon, he was brought before King Saul. Saul said, "You cannot fight Goliath. He is a trained man of war!"

Hearing this, David said to Saul, "I am not afraid to fight with Goliath! He made fun of God's army. So the Lord will help me kill this giant." Reluctantly, Saul agreed.

David took his shepherd's staff and a sling, and hid five smooth stones in his pouch. He then went to confront Goliath. Goliath was furious to find an unarmed boy accepting his challenge. He tried to mock him. But David replied that the Lord would defeat him without the help of any weapon.

As Goliath moved closer, David took out his sling and aimed a stone at the giant's forehead. Goliath fell to the ground. Then, David drew out the giant's own sword, and killed him.

At once, the Philistines turned to escape to their own land but the Israelites chased them and killed them. And David became Israel's hero!

Jonathan's Friendship Saves David

Long before David encountered Goliath, he was the harp player and armour bearer for King Saul. David had killed Goliath with God's help. And he became a hero overnight!

Saul made David an officer among his soldiers. David was wise and brave. However, David's popularity made Saul jealous. He thought constantly that David might try to replace him as the king of Israel.

All these thoughts made Saul unhappy. So David played his harp to soothe him. Twice Saul threw his spear at David. But David escaped each time!

Soon, Saul became obsessed with the desire to kill David. He began sending David for dangerous wars. But David came home safely every time.

One day, Saul promised David his daughter's, Michal, hand in marriage if he killed a hundred Philistines. David came back after killing two hundred of them. Michal loved David. Saul had to let her marry David.

However, Saul's son Jonathan loved David with all his heart. He felt very sad about his father's jealously of David. He warned David of his father's plans to kill him and urged him to flee immediately. Michal, Saul's daughter and David's wife, too helped David to escape.

Michal placed an image in David's bed and covered it with sheets so that it looked like a man. When Saul's servants came she said that David was sick. Soon, Saul found out that David had got away.

Later, David met Jonathan who promised to warn him with arrows. After three days, Jonathan went near the pile of stones where David was hiding, and shot arrows. He called out to his young helper, "The arrow went far beyond you! Hurry! Go quickly!" This was a signal for David that his life was in danger. After some time, David came out of his hiding place. The two friends hugged and parted ways. In time, David became the greatest king that Israel had ever known!

Solomon Asks to Be Wise

Solomon was the fourth son of King David. When David was on his deathbed, he had assured his wife, Bathsheba, that Solomon would be his successor. Even God favoured Solomon!

Solomon was very young when he was anointed the King of Israel. Before David died, he had told his son to obey God always and be a good king. Though Solomon had a good heart, he realised that he was too inexperienced to rule over the great nation of Israel.

So Solomon went to the holy place at Gibeon and offered sacrifices to the Lord. Finally, God appeared to him in a dream and told him to ask for anything he wanted. Solomon asked for a wise heart so that he could know the difference between right and wrong.

God was pleased with Solomon's choice. He blessed him not only with wisdom but also with riches and honour. Solomon became a great king. People from all over the world visited his court.

One day, two women came to Solomon's court and claimed that they were the mother of a baby. They said they lived in the same house and had babies around the same time. But when one of the babies died, both the women wanted the baby that was alive. King Solomon thought for a while. He had a plan he asked his guard to cut the baby into half and give one half to each woman.

To save the baby, the real mother said that the other woman could have the baby. He handed the baby to the real mother, as he knew she was the real mother.

All of Israel understood that King Solomon had indeed been blessed by the Lord.

77

Solomon Builds God's Temple

King David wanted to build a temple for God in Jerusalem to keep the sacred Ark of Covenant. Over time, he had gathered a great treasure of gold, silver, wood, brass and iron.

But God forbade David from doing so because he was a 'man of wars'. God wanted a 'man of peace' to build the temple. So, He chose David's son, Solomon, for the purpose.

After four peaceful years of reign as king, Solomon decided to start building the temple of God. He built it exactly like God wanted. It was built with praise, prayer and quietness. It had the best of every material and was built by the most skilled craftsmen.

Thousands of people helped build the temple. It took seven years to complete the construction. And it was a sight to behold! The temple was huge and well-decorated, solid and strong. It was grander than any palace or building.

The day the temple was dedicated to God was a day of great celebration in Israel. Everyone was invited for the function. The priests placed the Ark of the Covenant inside the temple. Suddenly, God's presence filled the temple with a cloud! Solomon then knelt before the altar, lifted his arms to heaven and prayed to God to bless the Israelites with His mercy and goodness forever.

Solomon then turned to his people and asked them to dedicate themselves again to God's service. He then offered special sacrifices to God.

Sometime later, God appeared to Solomon in a dream, and said that his prayer was heard. He promised to bless him and the Israelites if they served Him truly. He also warned that He would leave the temple forever if they turned to other gods.

Boy King finds Lost Book of Law

Israel's last good king, Josiah, was just eight years old when he inherited the throne of Judah. His ancestors had encouraged worship of false gods and idols in the Lord's Temple at Jerusalem.

Josiah loved God with all his heart. He was horrified to see God's temple in ruins. He wanted his people to serve the one true God. So he sent men throughout his kingdom to break down the altars and images of the false gods.

When he turned eighteen, he commanded that the people contribute towards the repair of the temple of Jerusalem. He also held the Passover.

During the restoration work, one of his advisors discovered the Book of the Law. Over the years, it had been lost within the temple.

When Josiah heard what was written in it, he was very upset. He knew, at once, just how far away from God his people had gone.

Then, Josiah read out God's Law at the temple where everyone had gathered. He then promised to love and worship God with all his heart and soul. All the people promised they would obey God, too.

Bold and Beautiful Queen Esther

A beautiful girl named Esther lived in Persia during the reign of King Xerxes alias Ahasuerus. After her parents died, her cousin, Mordecai, took care of her and raised her as his own daughter.

King Xerxes fell in love with Esther, and made her his queen. Everyone liked Esther, but she had a secret! She was an Israelite!

King Xerxes had an official named Haman. He was more powerful than anyone in the kingdom. The king had given him a seat of honour, meaning everyone had to bow down when Haman walked past him! However, Mordecai refused to bow because he worshipped only God.

One day, Haman noticed Mordecai was not respecting him. Haman was enraged! He found out that Mordecai was an Israelite. He thought of a way to kill Mordecai and the other Israelites. One day, he tricked King Xerxes into signing a decree to put all the Israelites to death. Not knowing that his wife Esther was an Israelite, the king passed the law and set the date!

When Mordecai learnt about this, he sent a message to Queen Esther and asked her to plead before the king for the lives of her people. Esther had an idea. She invited the king and Haman to a banquet that day. At the banquet, Esther invited them to another banquet the next day.

The king soon found Mordecai had once saved his life, and wanted to reward him for his good actions. The king again asked the queen at the banquet what she desired. Pointing to Haman, the queen revealed that they had been sold to be slaughtered by Haman. She pleaded for her life and the life of her people.

The furious king ordered Haman to be hanged on the gallows that he had prepared for Mordecai. He also passed an order to overrule Haman's wicked plan to destroy the Israelites. He then honoured Mordecai who made a new law to save all the Israelites. Esther was able to save her people because she was willing to risk her life and go to the king.

Daniel Unharmed in Lions' Den

Daniel was a man of faith and prayer. He lived in Babylon that was ruled by King Darius. Daniel was one of the three men chosen by the King to help him to rule the kingdom.

Daniel was wise and loyal. King Darius planned to make him his successor. But the other leaders were jealous of Daniel, so they schemed against him. But they never found any fault with Daniel. The only thing they saw was his unwavering dedication to God. And they decided to use it against him!

They tricked the king into passing a law which said that no one could pray to anyone but King Darius for thirty days! Anyone disobeying it would be thrown into the den of lions.

Daniel knew of the law, but he did not stop praying. He knelt down by the window that looked towards Jerusalem and continued to pray three times a day, just as he had always done. The other leaders reported Daniel's disobedience to the king. King Darius was very upset but he had to keep the law he had passed. So Daniel was thrown into the den of lions.

The king hoped that Daniel's God would perform a miracle. That night, King Darius could not sleep or eat. At the crack of dawn, he rushed to the lions' den and called out sorrowfully to Daniel.

Daniel answered, "My God has closed the mouths of the lions. They have not hurt me. I have been innocent of any evil against you or my God."

The king was very happy and ordered Daniel to be freed. He then ordered to throw the false accusers into the same den. The hungry lions pounced on them at once and tore them apart!

King Darius then passed another law that everyone in his kingdom should fear the God of Daniel.

God Calls but Jonah Runs

God commanded an Israelite prophet named Jonah to warn the people of Nineveh and ask them to correct their wicked ways or face His wrath. But, Jonah did not want to preach there. So, he boarded a ship to Tarshish and went in the opposite direction.

Jonah's disobedience angered God. He immediately sent a great storm. Everyone on board feared that the ship was going to sink! They decided to cast lots to find out who was bringing such trouble upon them. The lot fell on Jonah! He realised that the storm was God's punishment. So he told the captain to throw him into the sea. Reluctantly, the captain threw Jonah into the sea. At once, the storm stopped!

But God sent a big whale that swallowed Jonah. Jonah prayed to God for forgiveness. But the whale threw up Jonah on the dry land only after three days. God talked to Jonah once again. This time, he went to Nineveh to preach. "You have forty days to repent. Else God will destroy your city!" he cried out all day.

The people of Nineveh at once, turned away from their sins and mended their ways. Even the king of Nineveh fasted. God forgave them.

But Jonah was angry with God. He didn't want God to spare the people of Ninevah. So, Jonah built a little hut on the outskirts of the city and sat down, waiting to see what God would do next. A plant with thick leaves grew next to Jonah's hut. It gave him enough shade from the sun. But the next day, a worm destroyed the plant! Then a hot dry wind blew, making Jonah miserable. He wished that he could die! But God chided Jonah for having more pity on an ordinary plant than the thousands of people in Nineveh who promised to live the way He wanted Jonah to realise that all living creatures were precious to the Lord. This was the lesson that God wanted to teach Jonah.

The Forerunner of Jesus is Born

An old priest named Zechariah and his wife Elizabeth lived in Judea. The couple chose to be faithful to God all their lives. They had prayed for a child for many years, but God did not answer their prayers.

One day, Zechariah was chosen to burn incense at the Lord's temple Jerusalem. He was standing before the altar when suddenly God's angel, Gabriel, appeared there. Zechariah was terrified!

But what Gabriel told him surprised Zechariah even more. Gabriel announced that Zechariah and Elizabeth would soon have a child. "You shall name him John. God has chosen him for a special mission. He shall lead many people of Israel back to the Lord," he added.

Zechariah did not believe that his aged wife would be able to bear a child. As a result, his power of speech was taken away from him until the birth of his son!

When Elizabeth was about six months pregnant, Gabriel appeared before a young woman named Mary in Nazareth. She was a cousin of Elizabeth and was betrothed to a carpenter named Joseph.

Gabriel told Mary that God had chosen her to give birth to the Son of God, the Messiah. Mary knew she was not yet married, but she trusted God.

Gabriel also told Mary that Elizabeth was soon going to have a child. She immediately set out to visit Elizabeth. When Elizabeth saw Mary, she was filled with the Lord's spirit. She knew that Mary would be the mother of the Messiah. Both the women praised God for His blessings. Mary stayed with Elizabeth for nearly three months before she went back to Nazareth.

Soon, Elizabeth gave birth to a son. When Zechariah was asked what name he would like for his son, he wrote the name 'John' on a tablet. At that moment, he began to speak, and praised God!

When John grew up, he became the prophet, John the Baptist. The purpose of his birth was to prepare the way for Jesus!

A Faithful Couple

Mary was a young Jewish woman who lived in Nazareth. She was engaged to be married to a carpenter named Joseph.

One day, Mary had a special visitor. It was none other than God's angel, Gabriel! He told her that she was favoured by God to become the mother of the Holy Son of God. "You shall name Him Jesus. He will be the King of the Kings and His Kingdom will have no end!" he added.

Mary was confused. She did not understand how she would conceive a baby without marrying! Gabriel assured her that she would become pregnant with a child through the power of the Holy Spirit. "Your cousin Elizabeth will also have a son despite her old age, as it is God's will," he added. She trusted God, so she believed the angel's words. "I am the Lord's servant! Let it be as you said," she said.

After Gabriel left, Mary went to visit Elizabeth and stayed there for three months. Soon, Joseph came to know that Mary was pregnant. Unwilling to disgrace her publicly, he decided to end their betrothal secretly. But God's angel appeared to him in a dream and told him to marry Mary without any hesitation.

"Mary will bear the Son of God who will save His people from their sins. You shall call this child Jesus," the angel told Joseph. Joseph was a man of faith, so he married Mary.

At that time, Israel was under the reign of Roman Emperor, Augustus Caesar. He had ordered that a census be taken of his vast empire. For this, the people had to go to their hometowns to get their names registered.

Since, both Mary and Joseph were descendants of King David, they had to enrol their names in Bethlehem. The journey to Bethlehem was long and tiring. It was especially painful for a heavily pregnant

Mary. When they reached Bethlehem, they found that the city was overcrowded. All the inns were full!

Joseph was worried about Mary's condition. Eventually, they had to take shelter in a stable. It was here that the Son of God, Jesus was born.

Birth of the Much-Awaited Saviour

Joseph and Mary had come to Bethlehem to get their names registered. But they could not find a place to sleep. At that time, Mary was heavily pregnant. So, they accepted a kind innkeeper's offer to stay in his stable. That night, Mary gave birth to a baby boy! She laid him in a manger, and named him Jesus.

Meanwhile, an angel appeared to some shepherds who were tending their sheep in the fields near Bethlehem. She told them about the birth of the Messiah and how they could recognise him.

Suddenly, more angels appeared and praised God. The curious shepherds immediately started for Bethlehem. They found the special baby in a manger and worshipped him. They soon spread the word of what they had heard and seen.

Three wise men from the east saw an unusual star in the sky and came to Jerusalem. At that time, Herod was the king of Judea. He was a very wicked king. The wise men visited Herod and asked him about the new King of the Jews.

Herod was troubled. He told the wise men to let him know about the baby. He claimed to them that he wanted to worship the baby.

The wise men were filled with joy when they found the baby in a stable in Bethlehem. They worshipped him, and gave him gifts of gold, frankincense and myrrh. They were later warned in a dream not to return to Herod. So, they left by another route.

Meanwhile, an angel appeared to Joseph in a dream and warned him about Herod's plot to kill baby Jesus. He told him to take Mary and baby Jesus to Egypt. Joseph obeyed the angel and left for Egypt. They stayed there till it was safe for them return to Israel.

Jesus is Baptised

Jesus was thirty years old when He left His hometown of Nazareth to start God's special work. Jesus wanted to be baptised. And He wanted His cousin John to baptise Him! So, He went to the Jordan River where John was preaching and baptising those who repented.

When Jesus asked John to baptise Him, he tried to refuse. John knew that Jesus was the Son of God who had been sent to save the world. He could not understand why Jesus wanted to get baptised. John said that it was in fact, he who needed to be baptised by Jesus!

But Jesus explained that John had to baptise Him for them to fulfil all that was right. John obeyed Jesus and baptised Him in the river.

The minute, Jesus was baptised, the Heavens opened. The Holy Spirit, in the form of a dove, rested upon Jesus. A voice from Heaven said, "This is my beloved Son with whom I am very happy."

The Holy Spirit then led Jesus into the desert. For forty days, He neither ate nor drank anything, and the devil tested him. Jesus answered him, using the written scriptures. The devil tried to tempt Jesus thrice. First, he tried to get a hungry Jesus to turn stones into bread. Second, he tried to make Jesus doubt God's power. Next, the devil tried to make Jesus sin against God by worshipping the devil. But each time, Jesus used God's words to resist the devil's temptation!

Finally, the devil left Jesus alone.

Jesus calls His Disciples

The baptism of Jesus marked the official beginning of His ministry. It was now time for Him to choose His disciples. He wanted to train twelve special disciples to continue His work after He returned to Heaven.

Once, John the Baptist was standing with his two disciples when he saw Jesus walking by. John pointed to Jesus and said that He was the Lamb of God. Immediately, John's disciples left him and started following Jesus.

One of the disciples was Andrew. After about a day, Andrew met his brother Simon and told him that he had found the Messiah. Andrew brought Simon to Jesus.

Jesus said, "You are Simon, son of Jonah. Hereafter, you shall be called Cephas, which when translated means 'Peter'." Peter became a disciple of Jesus.

The permanent call to follow Jesus was received on the Sea of Galilee when Andrew and Peter were washing their fishing nets. Jesus saw Peter and Andrew and asked them to follow him. He said He would make them fishers of men. They left their nets immediately and followed him.

Then, Jesus called two other fishermen, James and John, the sons of Zebedee. They too left everything and followed Jesus.

The next day, Jesus saw Philip and said, "Follow me." Jesus then called Matthew, the tax collector, Thomas, Bartholomew, James, the son of Alphaeus, Thaddaeus (also called Judas, brother of James) and Simon, the Zealot.

Judas Iscariot, who also lived closely with Jesus, was given charge of the disciples' money. He was a dishonest man. It was he who finally betrayed Jesus.

These disciples were called Apostles, and had authority and ability to cast out evil spirits and to heal every kind of disease and illness.

Jesus' First Miracle: Water into Wine

Once, Jesus went to attend a wedding in the village of Cana in Galilee, with his mother Mary and a few disciples.

After a while, Mary came over to Jesus and explained that the wedding host had run out of wine. Jesus replied, "Why do you involve me? My time has not yet come."

But Mary knew her extraordinary son would take care of the situation. She told the servants to do whatever Jesus instructed them.

Jesus told the servants to fill six stone jars with water. The jars were filled to the brim.

The water in these jars was actually used by the Jews to wash their hands and feet before meals. Then, Jesus asked the servants to serve some of that water to the steward in charge of the wedding.

The steward tasted the water. It had turned into wine! He called the bridegroom aside and complimented him, "Everyone serves the best wine first. But you have saved the best till now."

This was the first miracle Jesus performed. He was the Holy Son of God, so He had special power to change water into wine. The amazed disciples believed and trusted Jesus in a greater way.

The miracle also marked the beginning of His public ministry.

Authority over Evil Spirits

Once, Jesus lived in Capernaum, a city of Galilee, where he regularly taught in the synagogue on the Sabbaths. The people were amazed at His teachings because He spoke so confidently and with authority!

One day, Jesus was preaching in the synagogue when a man suddenly shouted at Him. Actually, the evil spirit within the man was using the man's voice. It had recognised Jesus and hence shouted, "What do you want from us, You, Jesus of Nazareth? I know you have come to destroy us. I know who You are, the Holy One of God."

Jesus spoke sternly to the evil spirit, "Be quiet, and come out of him." The evil spirit shook the man violently, gave a loud shriek and left.

The people who watched this were astonished. They spoke among themselves about how Jesus commanded an evil spirit with authority to obey Him. Soon, the news spread all over Galilee. As a result, many sick and demon-possessed gathered at Peter's house to be healed by Jesus.

Once, Jesus and His disciples went to Gerasenes where they met a man with an evil spirit. This man lived in a cemetery by the Sea of Galilee. He wandered through the tombs without clothes day and night, screaming and cutting himself with stones. People tried to chain him down, but he was so strong that he broke the chains!

The man knelt before Jesus and started talking in a very strange voice. The demon confessed that there were many of them within the man and begged Him not to hurt them. Jesus then sent the demons into a herd of 2,000 pigs. The pigs rushed into the Sea of Galilee and drowned!

The swineherds ran into the town to tell everyone what had happened. The people rushed to the shore and saw the impossible. The demon-possessed man was sitting with Jesus. He was in his right mind and dressed! Afraid, they asked Jesus to leave their region. Jesus agreed, but asked the man whom He had healed to go and spread His word.

Calming the Storm

After preaching all day, Jesus wanted to have a quiet evening to Himself. He got on a boat and asked the disciples take Him to the other side of the Sea of Galilee.

Suddenly, there rose a great and mighty storm in the sea. The storm was so great that the boat was being covered with the waves washing over it and began filling up with water.

While the storm was rocking the boat, Jesus was fast asleep on a cushion in the stern. The disciples woke Him up and said, "Save us Lord! We are going to die! Do you not care that we are dying?"

He said to them, "Why are you afraid? Do you still have no faith?"

Then Jesus got up and commanded the storm. He said to the sea, "Hush, be still!" And the wind died down and the sea became perfectly calm. The disciples were amazed and said among themselves, "What kind of man is this, that even the winds and the sea obey him?"

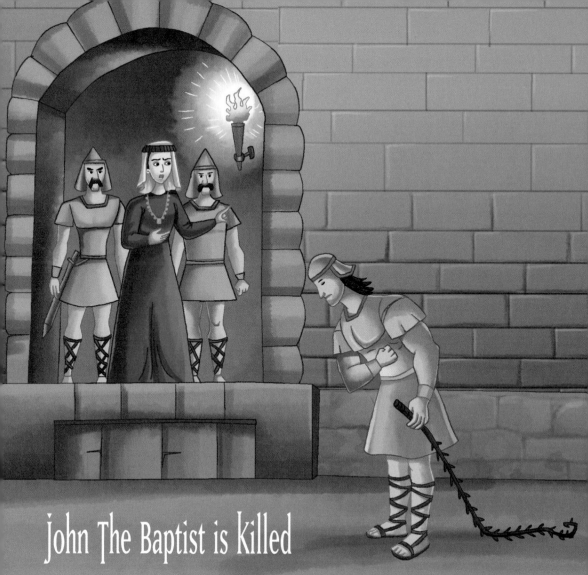

John The Baptist is killed

John the Baptist was a popular preacher who taught people to repent and turn to God. He also baptised those who confessed their sins. People wondered if he was the Messiah, but he clearly said that he was not Jesus Christ but was sent ahead of Him.

John was a fearless servant of God. He always spoke the truth which later cost his life.

At that time, the ruler of Galilee was Herod Antipas, the son of Herod the Great. He had married his half-brother Philip's wife, Herodias. John told Herod what he had done was wrong in God's sight. This angered Herodias. To please her, Herold threw John into prison.

But Herod did not dare to harm John. He knew John was a holy man and he liked listening to him. Herodias knew that the king did not want to anger his people. So, she devised a plan to kill John.

On Herod's birthday, a big banquet was arranged for the high officials and military commanders. At the banquet, Herodias' daughter, Salome, danced before the guests. Herod was so pleased that he promised to give her whatever she requested. Prompted by her mother, Salome demanded the head of John the Baptist on a plate!

Herod was upset, but he had promised to give whatever she asked. He ordered the executioners to behead John. They did so and brought John's head on a platter. Herod presented it to Salome who in turn gave it to her mother.

Feeding the Multitudes

Jesus was informed about the unjust death of His cousin, John the Baptist. He immediately withdrew to a place near the Sea of Galilee to be alone.

However, the crowds followed Jesus. They wanted to hear his words, and experience His love. When Jesus saw them, He was filled with compassion and healed them. He spent all day teaching the people about God.

Soon, it was evening. The disciples told Jesus to send the crowd away. They could eat and stay in the nearby villages.

Instead, Jesus asked the disciples to give the people something to eat. The disciples replied that a little boy had only five loaves of bread and two fish. They would need money to buy more food. There were about five thousand men; women and children had not even been counted.

Jesus instructed the disciples to make the people sit in groups of fifty. After they were seated, Jesus took the five loaves of bread and the two fish and prayed over them. He asked the disciples to distribute the food to the people.

Amazingly, after everyone had eaten there were twelve baskets full of leftovers!

The Lord's Prayer

Jesus always took time to be with God, His Heavenly Father. Bible narrates so many incidents where He had prayed alone, in public, before meals, before important decisions, before and after healing, among other things.

Once, a huge crowd had gathered to listen to Jesus. They sat on a hill, and Jesus taught them and His disciples the right way to pray.

Jesus told them how some people prayed in public places. They do so, because they want everyone to see them and praise them. Jesus said God wants people to pray in a quiet place in their own words. People should keep their prayers simple. God knows what we need even before we ask Him for those things.

Jesus told them that if they prayed sincerely to the Father in His name, their prayers would be answered.

Then, Jesus taught them a pattern of prayer, which today is commonly called the Lord's Prayer:

"Our Father in Heaven, blessed is Your name.

Your kingdom come, Your will be done on earth as it is in Heaven.

Give us today our daily bread.

Forgive us our sins, as we forgive those who have sinned against us.

Lead us not to temptation.

But deliver us from the evil one.

For Yours is the Kingdom, the power and the glory forever.

Amen."

Jesus Walks on Water

Following the miraculous feeding of five thousand people, Jesus sent His disciples on their boat to the other side of the Sea of Galilee. He then went up a mountain to pray. He stayed there and prayed till late night.

Meanwhile, the disciples had reached the middle of the lake. A storm arose and the boat began to be tossed in the high waves. Though some of the disciples were experienced fishermen, they too found it hard to control the boat in the storm.

It was very early in the morning when Jesus came down to join His disciples. He saw His disciples struggling in the wind. He began to walk on the water! The disciples saw this and were scared. They thought it was a spirit! But then, Jesus spoke to them, "It is me, do not be afraid."

Peter replied, "Lord, if it is You, call me to join You on the water." Jesus called Peter, "Come ahead. "Peter started walking on the water towards Jesus. But when he saw the stormy wind, he was scared and started sinking. He cried, "Master, save me!"

Jesus grabbed his hand and said, "Why did you doubt me? You should always have faith in me!"

Both of them then climbed into the boat and the storm calmed down. The disciples worshipped Jesus, saying, "Truly, You are the Son of God!"

Faith through the Roof

People who wanted to hear Jesus and be healed by Him longed to meet Him. When they heard He was in Capernaum, they thronged the house where He was staying. It was so packed that there was no more space inside or outside.

A paralysed man wanted Jesus to heal him and make him walk. So his friends carried him on a mat to the house. But they were very disappointed. Would they get their friend to Jesus through the overcrowded room? Suddenly, they had an idea!

The friends took off the roof tiles, lowered him and laid him before Jesus. Seeing the men's faith, Jesus said, "Son, your sins are forgiven."

The teachers of the law heard this and wondered among themselves who Jesus was. They knew only God can forgive sins, and to them Jesus was just another man.

Jesus knew their thoughts and asked them, "Is it not easier to say your sins are forgiven rather than saying get up and walk?"

Then, He informed them that the Son of Man had the right on the Earth to forgive sins. Turning to the man, he said, "Get up, take your mat and go home."

The man took his mat and went home, praising God.

It All Depends on the Soil

Once, Jesus was sitting by the Sea of Galilee when a huge crowd gathered around him. So He got into a boat and began telling a parable.

Once, a farmer went out to his garden to sow some seeds. He scattered some on the side of the road and the birds ate them up. Some fell on the rocks so the plants could not take root. The seeds that fell among thorns got choked. The ones that fell on good soil grew well.

Jesus explained the meaning. The seed represents the Word of God. People who hear the word of God, but allow Satan to snatch it away are like the seeds scattered on the side of the road.

The ones on rocky ground are like people who hear the word, but change their minds when trouble comes. The thorny ground represents people who hear the word, but they allow the worries of the world to make them unfruitful. The good soil signifies people who accept the word and bear good fruit.

The Man up a Tree Saved

Zacchaeus was a tax collector and a wealthy man. He had no friends because he cheated people. Once, he heard that Jesus was passing through his hometown Jericho, he longed to see Him. He was a short man, so he climbed up a sycamore-fig tree.

When Jesus reached the tree, He looked up and called out, "Zacchaeus! Come down now. I must stay in your house today."

Zacchaeus gladly welcomed Jesus into his home. The crowd murmured, "He is going to be a guest in that sinner's house." No one liked tax collectors because they became rich by cheating common people.

However, after Jesus spent time with him, Zacchaeus was a changed man. He promised Jesus to give half his wealth to the poor and return four times the amount to anyone whom he had cheated.

Jesus said, "Today, salvation has come to this house, because this man, too, is a son of Abraham, for the Son of Man came to seek and to save the lost."

126

A Centurion's Faith

Once, Jesus was walking towards Capernaum after His prayer at a nearby mountain. When He entered the town, a few soldiers of a Roman Centurion met Him with an urgent request. The Centurion wanted Jesus to heal one of his servants. The servant was so sick that he might die soon.

The soldiers said that this Centurion loved their country and had built a synagogue for them. So Jesus went with them towards the Centurion's house.

The Centurion felt he did not deserve to have Jesus enter his house. Neither did he consider himself worthy enough to visit Jesus. He sent his friends to tell Jesus not to trouble Himself to come, just speak the word and it would be done.

Jesus marvelled at what he heard. He turned to the crowd and said, "I have not found anyone with such great faith, even in Israel."

Those who carried this message returned to the Centurion's home and found the servant had been healed.

Jairus' Daughter Healed

A synagogue ruler named Jairus lived in Nazareth. He had a daughter who was very ill and was dying. She was his only daughter, and was twelve years of age.

When Jairus heard that Jesus was nearby, he went to Him, and knelt before Him. He pleaded with Jesus to come to his house and heal her.

Jesus went along with His disciples. But He had speak to the people who were waiting for Him. Suddenly, someone came from Jairus' house and told Jairus, "Don't bother the Teacher anymore, your daughter is dead!"

Jesus said to Jairus, "Don't worry, just believe and she will be healed."

Jesus went into the house with His three disciples. Many people were mourning for her. Jesus told them, "Stop mourning, she is not dead but asleep."

Then, Jesus took the girl by her hand and said, "Little girl, get up." The girl stood up.

Jesus instructed that something be given to her to eat and not to tell anyone what had happened.

The Unclean Woman

A woman who had been suffering from a rare disease for twelve years, lived in Nazareth. She had spent all that she had but no doctor could heal her.

One day, she heard Jesus had come to Nazareth. She went to see Him. She came up behind Jesus and touched the hem of His robe. Immediately, she felt she was healed of her disease!

But Jesus felt power going out of Him. So, He turned around and asked, "Who touched My clothes?"

Peter said, "Master, the people are pressing against you, many would have touched you."

The woman who had touched Jesus' robe knew she could not remain hidden for long. She stood up and fell at His feet. In front of everyone in the crowd, she told Jesus why she had touched the edge of His robe and how she was healed, instantly.

Then, Jesus said to her, "Daughter, your faith has healed you. Go in peace!"

The Blind Who Saw

The crowds liked to hear Jesus' teachings and be healed by Him. So they would follow Him everywhere.

One day, Jesus was walking away from Jericho when He saw two blind men sitting along the way. The men heard the chattering of the people and knew that Jesus was coming. They did not want to lose the chance to be healed.

They started shouting, "Have mercy on us, O Lord, Son of David!"

The crowds scolded them. "Be quiet!"

But the two men shouted even louder, to draw Jesus' attention.

Jesus heard their cries. He stopped and stood still. Everyone fell silent.

Seeing them, Jesus was moved with compassion. Jesus called them, "What would you like me to do for you?"

The blind men could not believe it! Jesus was actually speaking to them!

"Lord, that our eyes may be opened!" they begged.

Jesus touched their eyes. They, at once, received their sight. Joyfully they followed Him!

Dad's Faith Heals Son

Once, Jesus was coming down a mountain with Peter, James and John. They saw a huge crowd gathered at the foot of the mountain. They immediately knew something was wrong. When they reached the crowd, they saw some scribes arguing with the remaining disciples.

A man from the crowd then saw Jesus and immediately knelt before Him. He looked worried, but told Jesus, "Master, I brought my deaf and dumb son to Your disciples. He has an evil spirit, which makes him

138

fall, grind his teeth and froth at the mouth. He is very weak. But Your disciples are not able to heal him."

Jesus understood why the scribes were arguing with His disciples. He addressed the crowd, "Oh faithless ones! how long will I stay with you?"

The distressed father brought his son to Jesus. At that time, the boy had another fit. Jesus felt great pity. "Please have mercy and help us!" the father cried.

Jesus said, "If you believe, all things are possible!"

Immediately, the father cried, "Lord, I believe! Help my unbelief!"

Jesus commanded the spirit to come out, never to return again!

Again, the boy was thrown and lay like dead. Jesus lifted him up fully healed!

When the disciples questioned Jesus why they could not heal him, Jesus replied, "Such healing happens by prayer and fasting."

The Thankful Leper

Jesus was travelling along the border of Samaria when He came across ten men with leprosy. The lepers had sores and white patches all over their body. Back then, one could get infected with leprosy just by touching a leper. So, they were kept isolated from others.

These ten lepers had heard about Jesus who had healed many people. They thought Jesus could heal them too. They loudly called out to Jesus from a distance, "Master, have pity on us!"

Jesus saw them and said, "Go! Show yourselves to the priests."

141

In those days, the priest had to approve that the lepers were healed and clean. The lepers listened to Jesus and went to show themselves to the priest. On the way, they were healed! But only one of them, a Samaritan, came back to thank Jesus.

Jesus said to him, "Where are the other nine? Didn't they feel grateful? Get up and go, your faith has healed you."

The Woman at Jacob's Well

Once, Jesus was travelling through Samaria. Jesus was tired, so He sat near a well while His disciples went to find food. This was the same well that Abraham's grandson, Jacob, had built!

After some time, Jesus asked a Samaritan woman some water. The woman had come there to fetch water. She recognised that Jesus was a Jew and was surprised that He spoke to her.

Jesus said, "If only you knew who I was, you would ask me for water. I would give you fresh living water. Those who drink from this well will thirst, but those who drink the water I give will never thirst again."

The Samaritan woman asked Jesus for that water. Jesus knew all about her past and present life. Surprised, she thought He was a prophet.

Jesus explained that God was looking for people who would worship Him with their spirit and seek truth.

The woman said, "I know Christ will come and explain everything."

Jesus said, "I who speak to you am He."

The Good Neighbour

Once, Jesus was talking to a crowd when a lawyer stood up and asked what he must do to get eternal life. The lawyer's intention was to outwit Jesus.

Jesus said, "Love the Lord, your God with all your heart, soul, strength and mind; and love your neighbour as yourself."

The lawyer asked again, "Then who is my neighbour? Jesus told a story explaining who is a neighbour.

One day, a man was travelling from Jerusalem to Jericho. Some robbers attacked him, took all he had and beat him.

A priest walked down the road. He saw the traveller lying and went away. Then, a Levite came. He saw the wounded man and walked away.

A Samaritan came. He stopped and bandaged the man's wounds. He then put him on his donkey and took him to an inn. He paid the innkeeper to take care of him.

Jesus asked who the lawyer thought was a neighbour to the wounded one. He replied, "The man who showed kindness!" The lawyer realised Jesus' true power and glory.

Jesus instructed that the lawyer, too, should do the same.

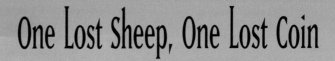

One Lost Sheep, One Lost Coin

The Pharisees and the scribes did not like Jesus mingling with the tax collectors and the sinners. According to them, these people were ungodly ones. To justify His action, Jesus told them two stories.

"A man had hundred sheep but one strayed away. The shepherd left his ninety-nine sheep and went in

search of the lost sheep. When he finds it, he will joyfully carry it on his shoulders and go home. He would call his friends and celebrate as he has found his poor lost sheep."

Jesus told them another story.

"A woman had ten silver coins. If she lost even one of the coins, she would light a lamp and sweep the whole house and look for it. She would turn the house upside down. Looking into every nook and cranny, she would not rest till she has found it.

"Then, when she has found it, she would call all her friends and neighbours, have a feast and celebrate.

"Similarly, there is great celebration in Heaven among the Angels when even one sinner repents over his bad ways and turns to God."

Jesus always shared great truths with the people through stories.

The Widow's Valuable Gift

It had been a long day for Jesus teaching, healing, and answering the Jewish leaders among others. So, He and His disciples sat down opposite the money box in the synagogue.

Jesus and His disciples watched as people dropped their offerings. They observed that the rich men made a lot of noise while dropping the money. They wanted to be noticed. Then, came a poor widow who quietly slipped in two small copper coins.

Jesus told His disciples, "This poor widow has given a bigger offering than anyone else!"

All the rest gave out of their abundant wealth, but the poor widow had given whatever she had.

Jesus was teaching His disciples the significance of offerings given for the work of the Lord. The offerings given out of a sacrificial heart have more value than money that is given out of excess.

Although the poor widow gave two copper coins, it was of great value because that was all the money she had.

Jesus' Transfiguration

Once, Jesus took Peter, James and John, and went up to Mount Tabor. Suddenly, the disciples witnessed Jesus' body undergoing a change. He was transformed from an ordinary man to a God-like being! His face was shining like the sun and His clothes were dazzling white as light. Then, Moses and Elijah appeared before Jesus and spoke with Him.

Peter was scared and told Jesus that he wanted to raise three tents, one for each of them to stay there!

A cloud enveloped them and they heard a voice, "This is my Son, whom I love, with whom I am well pleased. Listen to Him."

The disciples fell to the ground, frightened. They knew that Jesus was the Messiah.

Then, Jesus touched them and said, "Get up. Do not be afraid."

When they got up, they saw Jesus alone.

Jesus told them not to tell anyone about what they had seen until He rose from the dead. They wondered what this meant!

The Ungrateful Servant

Once, Peter asked Jesus how many times he should forgive someone if they committed any wrong against him. Jesus replied that he should forgive them seventy times seven.

Jesus further explained it with a parable.

Once, a servant had borrowed ten thousand gold coins from his master and was not able to return it. So, the servant begged his master for some time. The master had mercy on him and cancelled the whole debt.

Now, that servant met his friend who had borrowed only a hundred gold coins from him. The servant angrily demanded his money. The friend begged for time but the servant did not show any pity and got him thrown him into prison.

When the master heard this, he called the wicked servant and said, "You, wicked man! I pitied you and cancelled your debt. Shouldn't you have done the same?"

The servant was tortured in prison till he paid back the master.

Similarly, God will not forgive us if we do not forgive others.

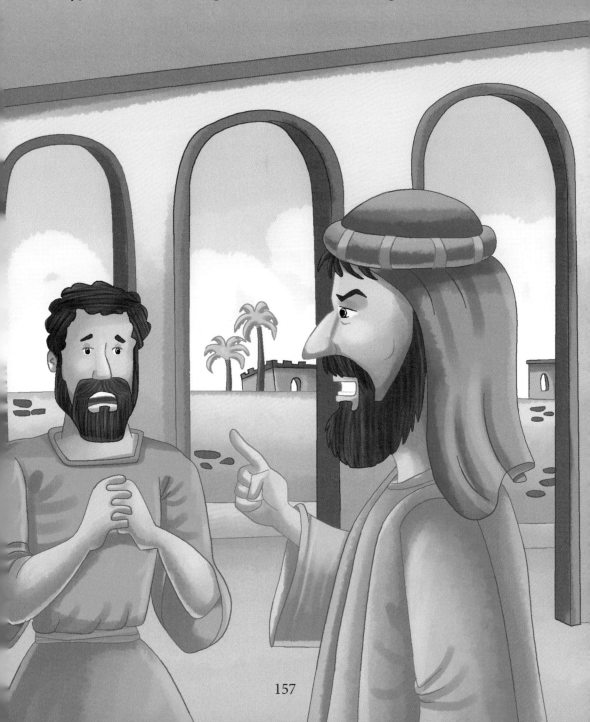

Little Ones are Special to Jesus

Multitudes followed Jesus everywhere. They liked to hear His powerful words about God and see His awesome miracles.

Now, the mothers in the crowd also brought their little children along. The mothers hoped that Jesus would touch them and bless them. Children too liked to be around Him. To Him, every single child was important!

But the disciples would get annoyed and chase them away. They thought the children were disturbing Jesus and His work.

Jesus was very angry when He heard this. He told them, "Do not push these little children away." He then enfolded the children into His arms.

Jesus continued saying, "Do not stop the children from coming to Me. The Kingdom of God belongs to those who are like children."

Jesus told all those around Him, "The truth is, unless everyone accepts the Kingdom of God like a child does, they cannot enter it. Whoever welcomes a child in My name, welcomes Me!"

Keep on the Watch

Once, Jesus told a story to teach the importance of preparing for His second coming. He compared the Kingdom of Heaven to ten virgins, who went to meet the bridegroom carrying lamps. Only five wise virgins carried oil in jars, along with the lamps.

The bridegroom arrived at midnight. The virgins woke up and trimmed their lamps. Then, the foolish virgins said to the wise ones, "Please, give us some of your oil; our lamps are going out."

The wise virgins replied, "Sorry! We cannot! We do not have enough oil for everyone. Go and buy oil for yourselves."

While the foolish virgins went out to buy oil, the wise virgins went to the wedding banquet. Then, the door was closed.

The foolish virgins returned and wanted to be let in. But, they were not allowed in.

Jesus warned people to be ready at all times. No one knows when Jesus will return to take His followers with Him to Heaven.

The Return of the Lost Son

Jesus was becoming more popular among the despised members of the society. This troubled the scribes and the Pharisees. They criticised Him about His closeness with the sinners. So Jesus responded to His critics by telling them a parable.

Once, there was a rich man who had two sons. One day, the younger son demanded his share of the inheritance. He then left home and wasted all his money, living carelessly. He had no food, so he accepted the job of a pig feeder. He was so hungry that he sometimes ate the pigs' food!

The younger son decided to beg his father for forgiveness. When the man saw his younger son at a distance, he ran and embraced him. He told his father that he did not deserve to be his son anymore.

But the man was so happy to have his son back that he forgave his mistakes instantly! He asked his servants to bring his younger son the best robe, ring and sandals and prepare a feast.

The older son, however, was so angry that he refused to celebrate his younger brother's safe return. The father pleaded with him.

The elder son said to his father, "Look! For many years I have worked hard for you! I have been a dutiful son. Yet, you never gave me a party like this!"

The father replied, "My son, you are always with me, and everything I have is yours. But we have to celebrate because your brother was dead and is alive again; he was lost and is found."

Through this parable, Jesus tried to teach that both the sinners and righteous are welcomed when they repent and turn to God.

Lazarus Lives Again

A Jew named Lazarus lived with his sisters, Martha and Mary, in a little village called Bethany near Jerusalem. Jesus was fond of this family and often visited them.

One day, Lazarus fell very ill. His anxious sisters sent word to Jesus and requested Him to come soon. They believed that their friend Jesus could heal their brother.

At that time, Jesus was far away from Bethany, preaching. So, He could not go to Lazarus right away. Finally, He reached Bethany. But by then, Lazarus had been dead for four days! Martha went to meet Him, and told him sadly that her brother would not have died if He had been there.

Jesus told Martha that Lazarus would live again. She knew that Jesus was the Messiah, the Son of God, so she believed His words.

Later, Mary came to meet Jesus, knelt at His feet and cried. Many people who had followed her, were also crying. Seeing their grief, Jesus too wept.

Jesus then went to the tomb where Lazarus was buried and asked the people to remove the stone that sealed the entrance. He then prayed silently and called out loudly, "Lazarus, come out!"

Lazarus, still wrapped up in the burial clothes, came out of the tomb alive!

Jesus' Entry as King of Israel

Jesus decided to go to Jerusalem for one last time to fulfil the prophecy of Zechariah—the Messiah King, who would come one day riding a young donkey. He knew that this visit could prove fatal, but it was God's plan for Him!

Jesus approached Jerusalem from the east and stopped at the Mount of Olives. He then sent two of His disciples to the village of Bethphage, and told them to untie a donkey and its colt, and bring them to Him. The disciples did just as Jesus had asked them.

The disciples spread their cloaks over the colt, the one that had never been ridden before. Jesus sat on the colt, and humbly rode into Jerusalem, as triumphantly as a king!

Hoards of people came out to welcome Jesus. They waved branches of palm trees and spread their cloaks on the path for the colt to walk on. They shouted, "Hosanna! Blessed is He who comes in the name of the Lord! Blessed is the coming kingdom of our father David! Hosanna in the highest!"

The triumphal entry of Jesus into Jerusalem is celebrated every year all over the world by Christians as Palm Sunday. It marks the beginning of the Easter Week.

Jesus Purifies His Father's House

A day after the triumphal entry into Jerusalem, Jesus visited the temple. But He felt it looked more like a flea market than a place of worship! The courtyard was filled with sacrificial animals and tables of the money changers. It was filthy and noisy everywhere!

To assist the people travelling from distant places, who wished to offer the Passover sacrifice at the temple, the religious leaders had approved the sale of animals outside the temple premises. Instead, they took advantage of the devotees and turned the house of prayer into a den of robbers!

Jesus was so furious that He decided to purify His Father's house. He chased all of them out! He overturned the tables of the money changers and the seats of those selling doves. He did not allow anyone to carry goods through the temple courts.

The chief priests and the keepers of the law were angry with Jesus. They wanted to have him killed as they were afraid of him.

The Last Supper

Passover is observed by the Jews every year to commemorate how God delivered them from slavery in Egypt thousands of years ago.

Jesus and His twelve disciples were in Jerusalem for the Feast of Unleavened Bread or the Passover. On the first day of the festival, Jesus sent two of His disciples to prepare the Passover Meal.

Peter and John were told to follow a man carrying a water jar. The man would lead them to the house where they would have the Passover Meal. Peter and John did exactly as Jesus asked.

In the evening, Jesus and the disciples sat for the Passover Meal. Before the meal, He washed the disciples' feet and dried them with the towel that was wrapped around His waist. By doing so, Jesus was imparting an important lesson—all are loved and treated equally by God in God's Kingdom!

Jesus then told them that this was His last supper with them. He revealed that one of them would soon betray Him. The shocked disciples wondered who it could be! Jesus said, "One among you who is eating with me!" He further explained that it was His destiny to die, but His betrayer's fate would be terrible.

Jesus broke the bread, blessed it and shared it with His disciples, "Take and eat it, for this is my body!" He then took a cup of wine, thanked God for it and said, "This is my blood. It will be poured out for you, so that your sins will be forgiven." As Jesus gave a piece of bread dipped in wine to Judas Iscariot, He whispered, "Do quickly whatever you are going to do!"

Every year, Christians all over the world observe the Thursday before Easter to remember the Last Supper of Jesus with His disciples. This Holy Thursday is known as Maundy Thursday.

Betrayed by a Kiss

Soon after the Last Supper, Jesus and His disciples went to the Garden of Gethsemane. It was an olive grove located on the Mount of Olives.

Jesus took Peter, James and John along with Him deeper into the dark garden. The other eight disciples waited near the gate of the garden. As He approached the garden, He told Peter, James and John, "I am sad and my heart is sorrowful, even to the point of death. Wait here! Keep watch and pray."

Jesus then walked ahead to a secluded place and knelt down. "Heavenly Father, let this cup of sorrow pass from me. But I want to do what pleases you," He prayed.

Jesus went back to His disciples and found them fast asleep. He woke them up and asked, "Couldn't you stay awake for even an hour?" He went back and prayed twice more. The disciples continued to sleep! He woke them, saying, "The time has come for me to be betrayed. The one who will betray me is ready."

The disciples then saw a large crowd of armed people approaching them. They could not believe their eyes when they saw Judas Iscariot among them. They understood that he was the traitor about whom Jesus had spoken of during the Passover Meal. Judas rushed forward and tried to kiss Jesus. This was the signal for the soldiers to recognise Jesus!

But Jesus asked Judas how he could betray the Son of Man with a kiss. He then revealed Himself to the soldiers. At once, the soldiers rushed forward and surrounded Him.

Peter was angry. He grabbed his sword and struck the ear of a priest's servant, Malchus. Jesus told Peter sternly to put his sword away. He then healed Malchus' ear. This was His last miracle!

The soldiers arrested Jesus and led Him to the house of the high priest. The three disciples ran away in fear, thus fulfilling Jesus' prediction and Zechariah's prophecy 'Strike the shepherd and the sheep will scatter'!

Peter Denies Knowing Jesus

Peter, James and John watched helplessly as the soldiers arrested Jesus at the Garden of Gethsemane. Then, they fled in fear. But after a while, Peter and John followed Jesus from a safe distance.

John knew the high priest, so he was able to let Peter into the high priest's courtyard. It was a cold night and some of the guards started a fire in the courtyard. He moved to stand near the fire so that he could see Jesus without being noticed.

Suddenly, a woman recognised Peter and shouted that he had been with Jesus. But Peter was afraid and confused. So he said, "Woman, I don't know Him!"

As Peter crossed the courtyard, a man said, "You are one among His followers." Again, Peter said, "I don't even know the man!"

As Peter was trying to leave the courtyard, another man said, "Surely you are the prisoner's follower. You talk like a Galilean!"

This time, Peter was angry. He cursed and shouted, "I don't know what you are talking about." Just then, he heard a rooster crow! At that moment, Jesus turned and looked straight at Peter.

At once, Peter remembered what Jesus had told him the previous evening that he would deny knowing Him three times before the rooster crowed! At that time, Peter had bragged that he would stick with Jesus even in the face of death.

Peter was very sad at breaking his promise to his Master. He went outside and wept bitterly.

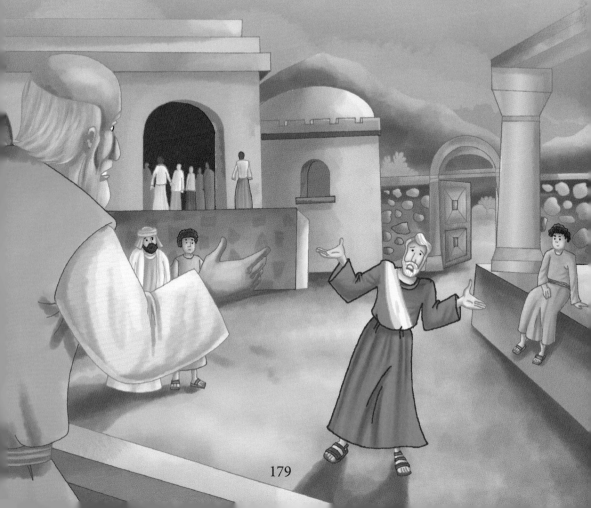

Jesus Stands Trial

Annas, a former high priest and the father-in-law of the current high priest Caiaphas, was the first to question Jesus. But Jesus saw through Annas' questioning. So, He refused to answer any questions about His disciples.

Jesus however said, "I have always spoken in the open. Why question me? Ask those who have heard me. They surely know what I said!" Jesus' answer offended a soldier who struck Him hard.

Soon, Jesus was brought before Caiaphas. There, the scribes and the Pharisees accused Jesus of false charges, but they could not find any strong evidence or witness against Him.

Throughout these proceedings, Jesus was silent. Finally, Caiaphas asked Him if He was Christ, the Son of God.

Jesus replied, "I am."

"That settles the matter," Caiaphas said.

Meanwhile, Judas Iscariot who had betrayed Jesus for thirty pieces of silver regretted his actions. When he realised that there was nothing he could do to save Jesus, he threw the thirty silver coins on the temple floor and hurried out. He later ended his sinful life!

The Jewish priests had no power to kill Jesus. So they took Him to Pontius Pilate, the Roman Governor who could sentence him to death. They told Pilate the charges against Jesus. But Pilate felt Jesus was innocent. Even Herod who governed Galilee could not find Jesus guilty.

Pilate knew that Jesus had not done anything worthy of death. The more he tried to release Jesus, the more the angry crowd demanded that Jesus be crucified and a murderer named Barabbas set free.

Finally, Pilate yielded to the people's demand. He ordered the crucifixion of Jesus. He then publicly washed his hands and proclaimed that he had nothing to do with an innocent's death.

The Saviour's Great Sacrifice

Bowing to public pressure, Pilate reluctantly sentenced Jesus to be crucified.

The Roman soldiers took Jesus into the palace and whipped Him. They then removed his dress and put an old purple robe on Him. They made a crown of thorns and pressed it onto His head. They then saluted Jesus and made fun of him by saying, 'Hail, the King of the Jews'. They also hit Him repeatedly on the head with a reed and spat on Him. All the while, Jesus never said a word!

The soldiers then dressed Jesus in His own clothes again and took Him out to be crucified. They put a huge wooden cross on His back and made Him carry it to a hill called Golgotha, meaning 'place of a skull'. A huge crowd followed them.

Unable to bear the weight of the heavy cross, Jesus fell down. The soldiers then ordered a man named Simon of Cyrene to carry the cross for Jesus until Golgotha.

At Golgotha, the soldiers took off Jesus' clothes again and gambled to see who got to keep them. They then nailed His wrists and feet to the cross and put a small plank that read 'The King of the Jews' on it. Jesus was then hung in between two thieves.

While hanging on the cross, Jesus prayed for others. He asked His Heavenly Father to forgive His tormentors. He then asked his favourite disciple, John, to take care of His mother Mary.

It was the middle of the day, but darkness covered the land. After suffering on the cross for many hours, Jesus finally surrendered to the will of God. He died for the sins of the entire world!

Jesus Rises from the Dead

Immediately after Jesus died, certain frightening events happened on Earth. The curtain in the temple of Jerusalem ripped into half, from top to bottom, on its own. A few days after His death, a powerful earthquake shook the ground. Huge rocks broke into pieces. Tombs opened and many saints came back to life.

People were very scared. A Centurion who was in charge of the other soldiers, said, "This man was surely the Son of God!"

On Pilate's command, a soldier broke the legs of the two thieves. This was done to speed their deaths. But since Jesus had already breathed His last, the soldier pierced Jesus' side with a spear. Blood and water flowed out of His body!

Later, Joseph of Arimathea and Nicodemus took Jesus' body down, embalmed it with myrrh and aloes, and wrapped it in linen clothes. They laid Him in a new tomb in a garden and sealed the top with a huge stone.

Two days after His burial, Mary Magdalene and a few women went to Jesus' tomb to place some spices around His body. But they were shocked to find the huge stone rolled away from the tomb! Jesus' body was also missing! At once, they ran to tell Jesus' disciples. Little did they know that Jesus had risen! Peter and John went inside the tomb and believed what they saw. They went away, rejoicing.

Soon, Mary returned to the tomb and peered inside the tomb. Two angels standing there asked her why she was crying. "Because they have taken away, my Lord," she replied.

Suddenly, she saw a man whom she thought was a gardener, standing behind her. It was Jesus Himself! Thus, Mary became the first person to see the Risen Lord, and announce His resurrection to His disciples.

Later, Jesus appeared before the other women who had come with Mary Magdalene to his tomb. They were on their way to tell Jesus' other disciples about His resurrection when they met the risen Jesus. He told them to tell the disciples to meet Him at Galilee.

Disciples see their Risen Master

On the same day, two followers of Jesus left Jerusalem and walked to a village called Emmaus. They were sad and were talking about Jesus. On the way, they were joined by a stranger. It was Jesus Himself, but the followers could not recognise Him.

Jesus asked, "What are you talking about?" One of the followers named Cleopas answered, "Don't you know what has happened here the past few days? Our master, Jesus, has been put to death."

The followers then narrated all that Jesus had done and how He had been crucified and now risen!

Jesus answered gently, "Didn't the scriptures tell you that Christ should suffer, and die for the sins of other people?"

Jesus then explained the scriptures, beginning from Moses, telling them about all the things what had been foretold about Him. When they reached Emmaus, Cleopas invited Him to stay the night. During supper, Jesus took the bread, blessed it, broke it and gave it to them. Immediately, they recognised that the stranger was Jesus himself. But He vanished!

At once, they returned to Jerusalem, found the disciples and told them that they had seen the Lord! Later, the disciples and some of Jesus' followers went together in a room the door of which they had closed. Suddenly, they saw Jesus standing before them. He said, "Peace be unto you!"

Jesus had appeared twice before His disciples. That was because Thomas had doubted that He had risen. Jesus looked at him and said, "You may touch the nail marks on my hands and feet, and feel the place where the spear had pierced my side. But stop doubting, Thomas!"

When Thomas saw the wounds, he was overjoyed to see his Lord alive.

He was also ashamed of his doubt. Later, Jesus ate with His disciples. The disciples were glad to see their Lord and were filled with wonder. "You believe that you have seen me," said Jesus. "Peace be to you, as my Father has sent me, even so I send you. May the Spirit of God come upon you."

Jesus Leaves for Heaven

Jesus Christ had appeared to His disciples for forty days after He had risen from the dead! Now it was time for Him to return to His Heavenly home. He had finished His work on the Earth.

As Jesus and His eleven disciples walked to the Mount of Olives, the place of His ascension, He gave His last instruction. He told them about the Kingdom of God and told them to stay in Jerusalem to receive the power of the Holy Spirit. He wanted them to tell everyone how He had died for them. He asked the disciples to teach and baptise all those who believed in Him.

Then, Jesus was taken to Heaven right before the disciples' eyes. A huge cloud hid Him from their sight and they could not see Him anymore!

Suddenly, two angels appeared and assured them that Jesus would come back again, someday, in exactly the same way that they had seen Him go up to Heaven.

A Glimpse of God's Beautiful Home

The night before Jesus was crucified, Jesus had told His disciples about His Father's household. He told them that He had to leave the Earth soon so that He could prepare a place for those who would eventually follow Him to Heaven.

In Revelation, the last book in the Bible, Apostle John shared a wonderful vision of a new Heaven. He saw the Holy City, called 'The new Jerusalem', descending from Heaven like a 'bride adorned for her husband'.

The angel explained that no sun or moon will be required, for God's own glory will make Heaven bright. There is no night at all. The length,

breadth and height of the Heavenly city are equal. The city itself is made of pure gold, like clear glass. The city wall is made of jasper. The city's twelve foundation layers are made of precious stones. There are twelve gates, each made of a single pearl, with an angel at each gate. There is a street of pure gold.

The crystal clear River of Life flows from the throne of God. The Tree of Life produces twelve kinds of fruit, none of them forbidden! The leaves are for the healing of the nations. No illness, pain or tears can ever exist there. No sin of any kind will be seen there.

All those who believe in Jesus Christ as their Saviour and obey Him will live with God in Heaven forever.